FIRE THAT COULD JUMP THE OCEAN

by

Tom Scarrella

Fire That Could Jump The Ocean
ISBN-10: 0989882802
ISBN-13: 978-0-9898828-0-4
Copyright © 2009 Tom Scarrella

Published by
Tom Scarrella Ministries
Fort Lauderdale, FL

Visit our Website at
www.SHAREtheFIRE.org

FOREWORD

Revival and fire go together like water and wet. In this book, Tom Scarrella chronicles three outbreaks of revival fire – Charles Parham in Topeka, Kansas; Evan Roberts in Wales; and then Azusa Street with Daddy Seymour. Fire is the number one essential ingredient in the Christian life. The fire of God is the passion, motivation and power to accomplish the will of God.

John the Baptist referred to Jesus when he said, "I will baptize with water, but there is coming one after me who will baptize you with the Holy Ghost and fire." This is why Jesus told His disciples to go and tarry at Jerusalem… until they were endued with power — fire-power — power to be a witness. We cannot do without the mighty baptism in the Holy Ghost and fire!

In my own life, I cherish that day in July of 1979 when the fire of God fell on me. Where would I have been, had He not touched me? I encourage you to read this book prayerfully and cultivate a spiritual hunger in your heart and life, just like Tom and Susie have, and then allow the fire of God to burn and continue to burn in your heart!

Dr. Rodney M. Howard-Browne
The River at Tampa Bay Church
Tampa, FL; USA

SPECIAL THANKS

A special thanks to Roberts Lairdon Ministries for their generosity in allowing us to use many of the pictures you've seen throughout this book.

A special thanks to the Baxter Springs Historical Society Museum and its helpful staff who provided many priceless articles, stories and information about the man and ministry of Charles "Fox" Parham.

DEDICATIONS

To my Lord Jesus Christ for saving me as a teenager and always being my best friend. Thank you for putting a fire of deep hunger for your presence in my heart.

To my beautiful wife Susie, who is always my inspiration and the love of my life. It's because of your constant encouragement that this book became a reality. Thank you for being my love and my princess.

To my son Paul, whose innocent and pure love for Jesus should be envied by all.

To my friends, Pastors Rodney and Adonica Howard-Browne, who've imparted into this generation a love for revival. In 1996 and again in 2002 my life was forever changed in your meetings when God's power ripped through my heart, changed my mindset and revolutionized my appetite from religion into a love for supernatural revival. I can honestly tell you that it was then when I stopped being a minister and I became a revivalist. I'm eternally grateful.

PREFACE

Why another book on revival? Most books about revival are full of names and dates and nifty stories of what God did yesterday or even centuries ago and all the while leave you looking back in history. I have a bit of a different take on things. I've always been that way I guess. Call me an optimist, I'm fine with that. My reason and purpose in writing this book about revival is to do more than just fill you with more dates, times and events of what God did "back then." The facts, names, stories, testimonies and lessons that are stamped on these pages will stir and empower you for the revival that God yet desires the earth to host. The coming revival is one that God wants YOU to experience and take part in – both through what He already has done and through the greater glory that is coming.

I don't negate the importance of past events. This is obvious enough or I wouldn't be writing a book about revival history. In many ways, I believe history has much to teach us. Remember when the man of God, Joshua, spoke from the Lord to the twelve instructing that each man should take from the River Jordan a stone?

> *"And it came to pass, when all the people had completely crossed over the Jordan, that the Lord spoke to Joshua, saying: "Take for yourselves twelve men from the people, one man from every tribe, and command them, saying, 'Take for yourselves twelve stones from here, out of the midst of the Jordan, from the place where the priests' feet stood firm. You shall carry them over with you and leave them in the lodging place where you lodge tonight.' "Then Joshua called the twelve men whom he had appointed from the children of Israel, one man from every tribe; and Joshua said to them: "Cross over before the ark of the Lord your God into the midst of the Jordan, and each one of you take up a stone on his shoulder, according to the number of the tribes of the children of Israel, that this may be a sign among you when*

your children ask in time to come, saying, 'What do these stones mean to you?'" (Joshua 4:1-6)

Those stones had a purpose. Those stones spoke aloud of a moment in history when God's people witnessed a great move of victory that would forever change their lives. That time when God displayed His power and glory wasn't a time to be forgotten, but remembered for generations to come. And now today we read about those times on the pages of our Bible in order to remember.

Those stones were stones of remembrance. So let me ask you the same question that Joshua asked the people of Israel that day, What do these stones mean to you? What do the stones of the revivals of the early 1900s mean to you? How much will you take from the lives of those brave and hungry men and women and then go beyond them into a greater outpouring of revival? Remembering is only step one. Reflecting upon the stones collected by the leaders of yesterday's revivals is important, but it's not the destination.

"...the Pillar of Fire is moving out again, and the Pentecostal people are so organized they can't move with it. God's fire will keep moving just like it did in every age. So don't ever draw boundary lines. It's all right to say, 'I believe this,' but don't end it with a period; end it with a comma, meaning: 'I believe this, plus as much more as God will reveal to my heart." — **William Branham**

There were three major revivals in the early 1900's that helped to shape Christianity to what it is today. Each of these revivals set a plumb line or a standard for believers to live by. They taught us the importance to desire after what God did back then and more importantly to deeply hunger for a greater measure today. Each of these revivals took place in very different locations surrounded by very different situations and led by very different individuals. One was a coalminer, another a farmer, the other was a city boy from the deep south.

As unique as each was, there was one common thread that knitted them together – a hunger for Holy Spirit Fire. While each leader was a contemporary with the very same fire of the Holy Spirit in their bones, they all learned that from their humility and teach-ability the Holy Spirit fire was accessible and His power could change their theology. They learned that His power could heal bodies and that power was so contagious that it could set ablaze the hearts of men and women around the world to burn with holy fervor and passion after the presence of God. As you read these pages, I hope that you too will begin to burn with that same hunger, humility and teach-ability.

CONTENTS

Foreword
Special Thanks
Dedications
Preface

Chapter 1   1
The Fire That Leads You is the Fire
That Feeds You

Chapter 2   9
It's Fire We Want and for Fire We Plead

Chapter 3   19
Conditions for Fire

Chapter 4   29
Fire That Could Jump the Ocean

Chapter 5   39
It Only Takes a Spark to Get a Fire Burning

Chapter 6   51
Feed the Fire

Chapter 7   59
Share the Fire

Bibliography   63
About the Author   65

CHAPTER 1
THE FIRE THAT LEADS YOU
IS THE FIRE THAT FEEDS YOU

"And the Spirit and bride say, 'Come!' And let him who hears say, 'Come!' And let him who thirsts come. Whoever desires, let him take the water of life freely." (Revelation 22:17)

In the summer of 1982 Brad came to my small western Minnesota town. He was a young adult with a vision to see God invade the young people of our region. He came with passion, zeal, and with the power of the Holy Spirit in his heart. He quickly started small bible study groups, one of which remarkably exploded in growth. Brad saw the outpouring begin. It started as a small group, only a handful of young people, but each of them were gloriously born again and empowered by the Holy Spirit. They grew spiritually and they began to see the gifts of the Spirit flow in their lives.

After months of small group ministry, Brad began to implore the youths to stretch their hunger for God in the two areas of prayer and evangelism. By praying in tongues weekly they called upon the Holy Spirit for the specific salvations of other young people in the school. It's doubtful if they fully understood what their leaders challenge had set in motion.

On a cool night in Morris, Minnesota, I was with my friends finding some sort of trouble to get into. Mischief was our goal and by golly we were going to find it. After driving up and down the main street a few times we grew bored. We ditched driving around and eventually ran into some kids from school. Little did I know that these were the fire filled youth from the bible study. It seems that they too were out that night in search of trouble, and they found me. Within moments one of the boys, Rodd, bluntly told me that I needed to be saved or else I would go to hell. I was stunned. After all, I was a good Lutheran. The initial shock wore down after a moment, but then I felt something I'd never felt before. It was strange at first, but I welcomed its coming. My body began to quietly shake and my knees were slightly buckling beneath me. I felt like liquid fire was traveling through my veins. Seizing the moment, Rodd blurted out, "Pray this after me Tom…" There I stood that night, in the middle of the street praying a simple prayer. How was I to know that moment would forever shape the course for the rest of my life?

Just a few months after I'd prayed that simple, but heartfelt prayer in the middle of Main Street I was introduced to the baptism in the Holy Spirit and in January of 1983 I was baptized in the Spirit and I spoke in tongues. Everything was new, and I felt power for the first time. The actual power of God that I could now use to change the lives of others just like Rodd used to change me. With excitement I would witness in school to the other youth. It wasn't uncommon for me to lay hands on the Evangelical kids for the Baptism of the Holy Spirit too. And if I found someone sick I would immediately minister healing. This thing inside of me was like an unstoppable force. The more I fed from the Bible, Christian books, tapes, and sermons the more it would grow. I even scripturally challenged my parent's Lutheran pastor, toe-to-toe, during a sit down meeting they'd arranged hoping to bring me back to my "normal" senses. But, it was too late. The fire had so taken over my heart and life and now there was nothing to go back to.

Since those early days of my Christian life, I have experienced that same fire again and again in very dramatic forms and fashions. It's been almost 30 years since I first touched the fire. My heart has been swept away with a love for revival history. My hunger for more of God's presence has given me a desire to learn how others experienced it too.

Like with any hunger I've come to learn that I must feed my heart that which it hungers for, and it clearly hungers for revival. I have studied and researched the lives and ministries of so many great men and women of God who have lived throughout the centuries. Although, each one unique, all shared that same hunger that lives within me today. They were touched with the same fire of God, and while their stories differ and the elements that surround their lives

2

are distinct, their end results brought them closer to the fire, which is always my first pursuit.

Charles Parham – His Childhood And Youth

In 1873, a man by the name of Charles Fox Parham was born in Iowa. When he was a young child his family moved to Kansas. Charles always had a love for God and for the things of God, but he struggled for years with sicknesses of many sorts. The worst of his ailments was rheumatic fever, which caused a lasting heart condition. Charles struggled with this until he realized that these sicknesses were a trick of the enemy, an enemy who was trying to keep him from the call of God upon his life. It was at this awareness that Charles had the revelation that God wanted him healed. So, Charles prayed the Lord's Prayer. When he reached, "Thy will be done on earth as it is in heaven…" Charles heard the voice of God say to him, "will you preach…will you preach?" From that moment forth Charles began to declare that he would obey the call of God and continued praying and crying to the Lord for healing. Reverend Charles Fox Parham later shared, "As I prayed, every joint in my body loosened and every organ in my body was healed. The disease was killed."

Two incredible spiritual experiences were credited for shaping Parham as a person and as a man of God. The first experience took place during a time of deep repentance at the young age of 13 years when he described a bright light that bathe over him. The second great experience was his severe case of the rheumatic fever and ailing heart condition at the age of 18 years. Despite receiving healing from God of the fever and the heart condition, the result of his sickness left him with a deep hatred in his heart for all manner of sickness and disease. It was this hatred that propelled within him a holy tenacity for healing the sick all over the world.

So much can be learned from Parham's insatiable hunger for the Holy Spirit and for his desire for the will of God to take proper place in his life. He was tenacious in fulfilling what God called him forward to, even in the midst of opposition, sometimes on every side. It was in his struggle that he overcame temptation including the temptation to avoid entering into ministry. Ministry wasn't Parham's first choice of profession. Parham longed and much preferred a pursuit of secular work in the medical field, but once again the fervent fire that burned within him required his stand against enticements to avoid entering ministry.

Like Parham and many ministers of the Gospel, I too have experienced temptation and have endured opposition on every side. It is that deep-seeded hunger and enduring tenacity for the Holy Spirit that has always won out in my heart, life, and ministry. And like Parham, I've learned to both yield to the Holy Spirit fire and to feed the Holy Spirit fire. What most Christians don't understand is that during times of opposition God is sculpting us. He molds us in order to fulfill our destiny. For years I wondered why certain individuals had it "easy" and seemed to have things and opportunities handed to them while I had it more difficult, fighting and crying out for mine. Call it maturity, but I've grown to realize that God was developing and challenging the revivalist in me, teaching me to endure in the midst of controversy and opposition. Charles Parham understood this too, and as a result he blazed a trail that no one in the 20th century had ever seen before. The perseverance and the art of hunger for the God's Holy fire was adapted by Charles and he was about to impart the same perseverance to those at the soon to be Topeka Outpouring.

Hungry for the Fire

Parham was consumed with an unquenchable desire for the manifestation of the glory of God in his life. This desire materialized in the start of Parham's first bible school, which he called, Bethel Bible School. The meaning actually translates, "the house of bread." He chose not to advertise the school, but prayed rather that God would draw students to it from different parts of the world. One by one, students began to arrive supernaturally at the school from the United States and Canada.

Many arrived with nothing except their Bible in their hand and hunger in their heart. Some where young and others older, both men and women, but each branded with the mark of Godly hunger. Parham was as surprised as anyone else about the turnout of students. Many testified that they'd been given a dream of a fire

4

burning in the middle of America. Clearly, this bible school was consecrated for the elite – for those whose desire was to experience more of God's power in their lives.

All too often in the church today we see apathy in the pews that's been propagated from the pulpits. A great example of that apathy was during a season of revival eruption in North America in the 1990's. Many church leaders were too comfortable to take the time to visit what God was pouring out to the hungry. The revivals of the 1990's were many times larger than what God did in the early 1900's through places like Wales, Azusa Street, and Topeka. Parham understood apathy and understood that the satisfied need not attend his bible school. Bethel Bible School was about raising and maturing a new breed of leaders – ones willing to go and do anything, at any time, no matter the God given request.

The unfortunate truth is that just as in the days of revivals gone by, the world is still full of mediocre ministers, and very few revivalists. Many charismatic believers love to study and learn all about the revivals of the past as they relax in the nostalgia, but few are willing to use what they've learned from the lives of others and become true vessels for revival who stand against the evil of the "status quo" in today's Church, pushing the spiritual envelope to a higher realm of the glory and grandeur of God.

Following through with his vision to open Bethel Bible School, Charles Parham proved his ability to be led by the Spirit of God. In a sense he heralded out to revivalists worldwide to come to the house of bread and enter into something no one in their lifetime had ever seen before.

Calling All Revivalists

So, where are the revivalists? Where are the men and women who are not concerned with filling notebooks or receiving the praise and accolades of man? Where are the strong, passionate revivalists who care less about inviting the next "big-wig" preacher to speak at their next big camp meeting or conference? Where are those who are willing to walk alone, if necessary, with nothing more than the fire of God burning in their hearts? It is only by the hands of these

5

extraordinary men and women who will blaze a trail forward, wrecking the religious golden calves in their path that have been built up by the pious religious for the masses to contently worship.

A true revivalist challenges lukewarm Christian television and gossip laden periodicals. They confront false doctrines that have run rampant from the pulpit down to the pews and are accepted by the majority. A true revivalist doesn't make for a good politician, but rises prophetically above the mediocre majority. The revivalist is not worried about their name flashing in lights and passing across the lips of widely known ministers, but they aspire to manifest as the sons of God with the pure river of life bursting through their churches and into the streets of their cities, transforming lives with the presence of our very powerful God.

Charles Parham was a revivalist and he did what precious few had done before him. He yearned and worked to develop nation shakers, history makers that would set captives free and break religious tradition. Today, the Holy Spirit looks among the mediocre majority to find for Himself the nation shakers, the history makers. As you read this now I sense your heart is screaming to be called out. Friend, the possibility is yours to be had. You've already been called and it's up to you to be chosen. Step forward and engage your heart to go after the fire of God, just like Charles Parham, and see your life and the lives of those around you shaken by the glory of God.

Preparation, Prayer and Healing

Parham's love for revival can only be exceeded by his love for prayer and healing. By forming Bethel Bible School, Parham had established a place to heal to the sick and a place to teach others how to pray and minister to others.

Parham grew up in a home where sickness was prevalent. Because of this, his disdain for sickness and disease was contagiously spread to his students. Parham and his students ministered with accompanying signs and wonders. Through times of opposition God was busy preparing a man to lead a new group of people who would be marked by hunger, prayer, Holy Spirit

6

empowerment, with a heart for hurting, sickly people around the world.

Parham understood an important key about Holy Spirit fire. He knew that he could not minister out of what he had never touched or tasted. Quite simply, you cannot minister the fire without experiencing the fire. Parham allowed the Holy Spirit fire to purge, purify, and prepare him.

Still Slaying the Prophets

Parham was known as a man with spiritual backbone and the ability to be forthright and blunt with brutal honesty. He pursued truth above all the accolades of man's praise. Religious leaders would often tell him that they too wanted the Holy Spirit outpouring, but behind his back they would secretly mock and ridiculed him. The Pharisee within them won out and as is customary it seems, the revivalist took the beating. Withstanding the numerous thrashings, time and again Parham would rise up stronger and more determined to see truth prevail. They simply could not slay this prophet to silence. This is what separated his ministry from the mundane and why we still glean from his ministry in the monumental pages of Christian history.

In 2004, my wife, Susie, and I relocated our entire ministry headquarters to Fort Lauderdale, Florida. We did so with an inward desire, a vision to see our region of the United States set ablaze with revivals fire. Four years later, in 2008, in our spiritual zeal we invited one of today's great revivalists, and our dearest friends from South Africa, to come and minister in a series of churches near our home and ministry headquarters. On the first night, this great man of God preached without compromise a strong message that was clearly not intended for the spiritually weak minded.

Undoubtedly, he hadn't traveled from around the world to powder the "spiritual bottoms" of those in attendance. He preached as he always preaches, with truth and powerful demonstration. As we sat there, hanging onto every word, our hearts were stirred afresh. Susie and I witnessed the local church leaders shout out their loudest, "Amen!" Their roars could be heard above the rest of the entire congregation combined. I thought to myself, this is great – even the church leadership here loves truth and are willing to yield to its demand for change.

I was so full of hope and excitement – until our dear friend left the building. As he exited we watched the Pharisee's within the leadership rise up to ridicule and mock. Later, we learned that one of the main financial givers in the church had taken great offense by the truth that had come forth against some false doctrine being taught at the church and that offense was just enough to turn up the Pharisee and turn down the purging and perfecting fire of God. And to this day, that church continues to dwindle in membership and influence, yet the revivalist preaches on still.

Parham was a man before his time. While the voice and influence of those religious mockers and Pharisee ministries would never be read of again, Parham was feasting on a Holy fire that would lead his ministry into the annals of revival history and change the vocabulary of Pentecostals and Charismatic believers forever.

Chapter 2
It's Fire We Want
And For Fire We Plead

"For I will pour water on him who is thirsty, and floods on the dry ground; I will pour My Spirit on your descendants, and My blessing on your offspring." (Isaiah 44:3)

In the late 1800's, Charles Parham was in search of a building that would be suitable to hold his bible school and all night prayer meetings. Soon he found a beautiful mansion built by a man named, Mr. Stone. Years previous, Mr. Stone set out to build one of the county's biggest, most grandeur mansions for his wife whom he dearly loved. He spent millions of dollars to create the home for her; a home that he hoped would be referred to as "Stone's Mansion."

Instead a much different future would be held for Stone's extravagant dream. After completing only half of the mansion Mr. Stone ran out of money. No longer would the city people refer to his beautiful home as "Stone's Mansion," but instead history remembers it as "Stone's Folly" for his inability to finish such a palatial design.

The building sat vacant for almost ten years before Parham leased the mansion. Soon after, he formed Bethel Bible College. It was also at Stone's Mansion that Parham began his search for the truth of the baptism in the Holy Spirit. With only his Bible and day and night prayer meetings, Parham along with his forty students, grew desperate for the Holy Spirit infilling. Their hunger was not satisfied until the fire of God fell upon Parham and one by one each of the students, thus the beginning of the famous, Topeka Outpouring.

Parham, his wife, Sarah Thistlethwaite-Parham, and his sister-in-law, Lillian Thistlethwaite, were the three fire-starters of the Topeka Outpouring, eventually speaking at the Azusa Street Revival in 1906. Parham stood out among church and religious leaders. Churches all around began to hear about his ministry. One Pastor from Kansas City, Missouri, asked Parham if he would please come and preach in his church during the time between the Christmas season and the start of the New Year. Parham obliged the request, but before leaving the bible school in Topeka he deeply challenged his student by instructing them to diligently search throughout the scriptures and find the most common manifestation of the baptism in the Spirit. Upon his return the students eagerly shared their discovery. In their studies they concluded that the key manifestation found throughout the New Testament was that of speaking in other tongues.

An All Night Prayer Meeting

On December 31, the last day of the year 1900, Parham declared to his students that they were to pray through the night in search of the baptism in the Spirit. The students eagerly agreed and by the dawning of the New Year, January 1, 1901, they encountered the manifestation they'd sought to find. One young woman, Agnes Ozman, asked the man of God to lay hands upon her. Parham answered her sternly by saying, "If I haven't received the baptism in the Spirit, how could I lay my hands now on you?" In her childlike faith, Agnes suggested that God would honor their desire. With that, Parham stretched forth his hands to Agnes and laid them upon her. As he did, she abruptly erupted, speaking out in a foreign tongue.

This took place for hours. She would both speak and sing in this tongue. The other students present would later testify that Ozman looked to have a halo around her face. Agnes tried to communicate to them what she was experiencing. She tried to write it down on paper, but in her attempt even the writing on the paper came out in tongues. It was found out later, through a linguist, that she was speaking and writing in perfect Mandarin Chinese.

Interestingly, when Agnes spoke in tongues she spoke the language of man. Following her experience many others too received a known language, such as Swedish, German and even Japanese. At one point there were as many as twenty-one known languages spoken, recognized, and confirmed as authentic. Oddly, it's recorded that Parham did not speak in tongues until several days into the outpouring, but when he did receive they said he spoke and sang in tongues all night long.

What joy it must has been. If you've had the opportunity to visit a Charismatic Pentecostal church in the last thirty years you'll know just how common speaking in tongues is for our generation, but imagine the awe that they must have experienced in those moments when it was first poured out since the days of the Apostles. No doubt, this was a supernatural outpouring. In addition to speaking in tongues, many other supernatural signs and wonders also were commonly experienced, such as writing in tongues, trances, visions, and dreams. In fact, it is said that it was not unusual for them to see tongues of fire dancing above their heads as they spoke in other languages under the Anointing of the Holy Spirit.

The night that Parham finally spoke in tongues he said,
"God made it clear to me that He raised me up and trained me to declare this mighty truth to the world, and if I was willing to stand for it, with all the persecutions, hardships, trials, slander, scandal, that it would entail He would give me the blessing.' And I said, Lord, I will, if you will just give me this blessing. Right then the glory fell over me and I began to worship God in the Swedish tongue, which later changed to other languages and continued so until the morning!"

The Topeka Outpouring had erupted and Parham students were filled, one by one, until the glory of God had so filled them all that their hearts didn't know if they would live or die. They would share it with everyone that they would meet out in the streets and elsewhere. God used them to boldly declare this baptism in the Spirit. Parham taught his student that this manifestation of Holy Spirit infilling was given with a two-fold purpose — prayer and missions. It wasn't enough to pray, they had to give it away to everyone they encountered. Eventually, this belief carried them and their message to the nations.

When We Saw Topeka

After revival touched and changed my life so many years ago I wanted to visit the buildings, the people, and the destinations where mighty, supernatural outpourings took place. I wanted to touch the gravestones and soak in the residue of their ministries. Susie and I have visited the gravesites of William Branham, Kathryn Kuhlman, Smith Wigglesworth and others. We've touched the wooden buildings from the days of the Cain Ridge revival. We've entered in worship at the Angeles Temple in Los Angeles, California and John G. Lake's healing rooms in Seattle, Washington. We've wept at the Brownsville Assembly of God in Pensacola, Florida and prayed in the secret prayer room of Andrew Murray in Cape Town, South Africa. I stood behind the pulpit where the great Martin Luther preached the beautiful message of grace in Jena, Germany. We've heard the criticism of those who call us "revival junkies." There will always be those who choose to mock the hunger so deep within our souls, but all we can do is seek and keep seeking. I am reminded of the words of a certain woman who was desperate to be near the presence of God. She said, "If I can just touch the hem…" So, while others refuse the fire, we believe for and go after more. The way that we see it, these are not just buildings and gravesites. These are places where the very fires of heaven poured out and revival flowed through the lives of so many others.

While ministering in Humboldt, Kansas in September 2008, we couldn't resist our temptation to travel over a hundred miles out of our way, just to get a chance to visit the ground where the great Topeka Revival began. From the airplane we rented a car and drove straight to the place described to us only in the many books we'd read about the revival. Finally, we arrived in Topeka just before dusk. From our research, we hunted up and down the streets of Topeka for the exact location of the famous "Stone's Folly" mansion. As we drove up, we saw no mansion at all. Instead we discovered a large Catholic Church, school, and office space. Had we miss calculated? Could this be the site? We got out of the car and instantly sensed God's presence.

There Susie and I stood in the parking lot of this Catholic Church weeping under God's Anointing. It was the strongest Anointing in a location of revival that we have ever personally experienced. We both agreed that if this wasn't the location we'd set out to find that it was, at least, a place we were glad to have ended up. Since it was so late in the day we assumed the church buildings would be closed, but we tried anyway, making our way into the unlocked church we found a lone staff person busily working with her nose in mounds of paperwork.

We inquired about the history of the church and told her that we were looking for the place known as the Topeka Revival. She grinned and said, "I've heard the stories. You're not the first to visit here, but I'm told that Stone's Folly burned to the ground only shortly after the Revival back in 1901." She went on to explain that the Catholic Church purchased it many decades ago and that the only building still left on the grounds from Parham's days was located behind the church. That building used to be an orphanage owned by the Catholic Church. It's said that Parham instructed his bible school students to visit the orphanage and practice praying for the sick in that building. She remembers hearing of the many miracles that took place in that building so many years ago. Today that building still belongs to the Catholic Church and is home to the church offices.

With permission from the staff, Susie and I grabbed our TV camera and began to film what we saw there that day. Later, we aired the footage on our weekly television program, All For The Kingdom, sharing with the world about the Topeka Revival. As we filmed we wept, realizing that Parham and his students had no idea that they were creating a history that you and I could one day partake of. As the tape rolled, so did the many tears of joy and hunger as the glory of God was upon us both in that holy place. Even to this day when I think of those hours spent at that holy site I am moved and stirred afresh in my mind and spirit.

I've spent over twenty years of life in the full-time ministry. In these many years I've met and befriended descendants of Parham's group. I've heard the stories told of their relative, of their first experiences with the empowerment of the baptism of the Spirit. One lady I met shared with me about her great-grandmother who was among the very first to speak in tongues when Parham's group prayed for her after their move from Topeka to Houston, Texas. She said that her great-grandmother didn't know that it was possible to speak in tongues quietly. Her great-grandmother would dance around the kitchen table in the Spirit and prophesy over each family member in an attempt to say grace before their evening meals.

She can remember her great-grandmother praying in tongues so loudly that it sounded as though God was moving through their home like a cyclone. Once, while washing the dishes in her sink with the windows in her kitchen wide open she began speaking loudly in tongues, then singing a beautiful spiritual song to the Lord in tongues. After about an hour of cleaning and Holy Spirit prayers there was a loud banging on her front door. There stood her neighbor sobbing and weeping. The neighbor blurted out, "Whatever you have and whatever you are speaking came into my house and I heard it and I have to have what you have!"

After our time on the grounds of the Topeka Outpouring we traveled to find the place where Parham's body now lay. As I stood over his grave the presence of God once again flooded my heart like it had some 200 miles back in Topeka where it all began over 100 years ago. His gravestone was carved and shaped from a large stone in the form of a pulpit. Parham was still preaching, but this time from the cloud. Carved into the face of the gravestone pulpit were the words, "Founder of the Apostolic Faith Movement." Even in his death people honor this man of God for the fire he hosted as a vessel of heavens Anointing. Standing there at Parham's gravesite and having just visited the place of the outpouring in Topeka, we couldn't help but cry out to God, pleading once again for a fire like that of this great man.

Short-lived Fire in Topeka - Time to Move

Parham and the ministry team of students were spreading the fire of the Holy Spirit all over Kansas and Missouri. Then in 1904 they traveled to Galena, Kansas and awakened the interest of the people of that region. It is recorded that in just over three months, more than 2,000 people were healed and more than 800 were born-again.

The Topeka Outpouring Revival lasted only a short while and in 1905 Parham felt it was time to move the bible school and its students to from Kansas to Texas. Along their journey south they encountered many people who needed this empowerment of the Spirit. They never viewed the Holy Spirit infilling as something to keep for themselves. They would minister to dozens of people who were filled with the Power of the Spirit and held to the belief that the baptism of the Spirit was given for the purpose of receiving power to spread the Gospel of Jesus Christ all throughout the world.

The Move Back to Kansas

It wasn't long after Parham relocated his ministry to Texas that his heart desired to return to Kansas, where the fire had first fallen. By 1905 he moved the ministry to Baxter Springs, Kansas, a city located in southern Kansas and its population rested at a meager 1,000 residents. Even still, Parham and his student ministry team, lead over 250 people to salvation in Jesus Christ in just one week. Can you imagine what would happen today if 25% of your city population was born again within a week?

Revival wasn't limited to Topeka, Kansas or Houston, Texas or even to Parham and his group of hungry, radical believers. Hundreds of miles away God was moving through another man, John Alexander Dowie in Zion, Illinois. History remembers Dowie as a man of miracles who pioneered a revolution within the Church for healing and miracles. When Dowie heard about what was happening in the ministry of Charles Parham he hungered for an impartation of that Holy Spirit Anointing and infilling that he knew Parham could impart. He quickly sent word to Parham to come feed his hungry soul in Zion, Illinois.

Kansas and Beyond

As with many revivalists or revival ministry's there was controversy surrounding Dowie and the city of Zion, Illinois. When the city leaders heard about Dowie's invitation to host Parham in Zion opposition arose immediately and in retaliation city officials shut down every building and meeting facility within city limits in order to avert Parham from bringing the strange manifestation to their city.

Parham loved and lived for the Holy fire and he refused to steer away from the controversies or oppositions that the fire brought. He traveled to Zion in 1906 fully equipped to change the spiritual temperature and feed the hunger in the region. Despite the attempts of city officials to segregate Parham from use of all city buildings, he and Dowie pressed forward, resorted to hold the initial meetings in lay person's homes. One man, F.F. Bosworth, opened his home freely. In his humble home, attendance records were broken as the amount of bodies filled the home to capacity. Bosworth was filled with the Spirit there, as was his close friend an insurance salesman, John G. Lake.

From the home of F.F. Bosworth, these men would take revivals fire with them to minister to masses throughout the world. Bosworth's home had become so popular during the weeks of Parham's visit that multitudes of people would travel there years later to receive from him the Holy Spirit. His home, from then on, would be known as, "Central Tabernacle" and there hundreds received the baptism in the Holy Spirit.

After several weeks of ministry and impartation Parham went on from Zion, leaving the fire to burn in Illinois. He returned home to his family and ministry in Kansas.

"The one concern of the devil is to keep Christians from praying. He fears nothing from prayerless studies, prayerless work, and prayerless religion. He laughs at our toil, mocks at our wisdom, but trembles when we pray." — Samuel Chadwick

Charles Parham died on January 29, 1929. He was heralded as the leader and chief in Pentecostalism and was the first to believe and proclaim that the "Initial physical evidence of the baptism of the Spirit is speaking in tongues." Hundreds of believers traveled from many nations of the world to Baxter Springs, Kansas to attend his burial and to celebrate his life.

Although today, William Seymour and the Azusa Street Revival receive most of the recognition as the first outpouring of the twentieth century, that assumption is actually misguided. The Topeka Revival was the first outpouring of the twentieth century and was responsible for heavily influencing the great William Seymour and his ministry.

Despite his imperfect character and human flaws, we must never forget Parham's deep pursuit of the fire of God. By the grace of God, Parham touched every nation of the world right from the middle of the United States of America with little more than hunger, desire and passion. Modern church leaders have much to learn from the ministry and the man, Charles Parham. He practiced what he preached. He insisted in sharing one's personal, supernatural experiences with others and giving others their own personal experience with Holy fire. Parham could never be accused of self-promotion. He didn't build a grand building and implore the world to come see The Parham Show. Instead, he, like the prophet Isaiah said, "Here I am Lord, **send me**."

CHAPTER 3
CONDITIONS FOR FIRE

"As they ministered to the Lord and fasted, the Holy Spirit said..."
(Acts 13:2)

Revival may seem out of reach and some people, with good intensions, have made revival seem very complicated. There are hundreds, maybe even thousands, of "revival" books available that will offer up a variety of methods to "get" revival. Some say preach less and hype up the music. Others present a step-by-step guide to the ninety-nine steps to the sixteen dimensions of the seven laws of revival. What? [I'm exhausted just thinking about that read.] In all our travel around the world, preaching and bringing revival to local churches and believers everywhere, we get asked a lot of questions. The number one question we are asked on the topic of revival is, "The spiritual ground is hard here Brother Tom, how can we ever have revival here?"

Firefighters train for months to learn the many aspects of fire. How does it start? How does it burn? How to put it out? Any firefighter will tell you that there are necessary conditions to start a fire. Weather plays a vital part in the starting of a fire and the fighting of a fire. Lack of water is another. The condition of the land can also affect whether a fire will ignite and how quickly it will consume everything in its path.

The same is true when it comes to the conditions for spiritual fire. Great men and women of God, such as Charles Finney, Kathryn Kuhlman, Charles Parham, John Alexander Dowie and Evan Roberts, each encountered such conditions. Shortly after the turn of the twentieth century the spiritual climate of Europe, especially the country of Wales, was an infection of carnality in the local church. Worldliness, hypocrisy and "going through the spiritual motions," had become an epidemic in the Church. While in this hotbed of sin and wickedness, many would argue that the Christian churches of Wales were far from ready to host revival, but the truth is that they were ripe and prime for an ignition. The spiritual wood was so dry at that time that even the smallest spark could ignite a great flame. It simply needed a spark.

"Moreover the law entered, that the offence might abound. But where sin abounded, grace did much more abound." (Romans 5:20)

During this time in Europe no one, in or out, of the Church was aware of the fire that was about to erupt, forever changing Christianity in Europe and around the world. Good Christian folks were involved in their normal activities and life was routine. But much like Parham and his small group, there was a remnant in Europe growing hungry for the presence of God. This remnant was small and unknown to most, but it wouldn't be long before their names would be etched forever into the annals of revival history too.

"You'll know when revival has hit, because it will affect every area of society at the same time." — Dr. Rodney Howard-Browne, Nuggets of Truth from God's Word

Prayer Meetings Everywhere

Up until the early 1900's the country of Wales had always been known as the land of revivals and revivalists. In fact, in the century prior many great men of God traveled to the America's from Wales and its nearby regions and with them was the Holy Spirit. At one time, that part of the world was rich in the Anointing and outpouring of the Holy Spirit. By 1904 apathy had consumed the European Church. In February of that year there were small prayer meetings popping up throughout Wales. One prayer meeting was in the home of a young man named Evan Roberts. He would wake in the early morning hours and cry out to God for revival to once again come alive in his nation. During one prayer meeting Joseph Jenkins, a pastor, asked the people to share their testimonies. The air became still and silent. Then a young teenager, Florrie Evan, a new Christian convert, spoke and simply said aloud, "I love Jesus with all my heart." With these plain, uncomplicated words a supernatural hunger and repentance struck that little group and from there it spread through the country of Wales like a cyclone, as young people were

20

being swept into the Kingdom of God daily and all who reached out were touched by the fire of God.

Seth Joshua, a gifted evangelist began to experience stirrings in his meetings also. He wrote, "Revival is breaking out here in greater power – the young receiving the greatest measure of blessing. They break out into prayer, praise, testimony and exhortation."

Evan Roberts was busy preparing himself for the ministry. He was young, only twenty-six years of age and in seminary, but he hungered deeply for something more. Many weeks and months before the start of the Walsh Revival, which was brought through Evan, he would be awakened at 1:00 a.m. in the morning and would continue in prayer until 5:00 a.m., crying out in worship and prayer in the shelter of his home. How was Evan to know that his hunger and prayer-filled worship was laying the foundation for a nation-changing, revolutionary revival? Praying for revival was nothing new to Roberts. He had been crying out to God in prayer for revival since the young age of twelve, at which time he had begun working in the coal mines, which wasn't uncommon for boy's his age. It was during his years in the mines where he had a powerful, life-changing experience with God. One day, while working in the mine, there was an explosion. Evan's Bible was burned on 2 Chronicles, chapter 6 where King Solomon had been praying for revival. It was on that day that his deep search for revival begun.

"Just a line to let you know that I am on my way home for a week to work with our young people. The reason for this is the command of the Holy Spirit. He gave the command last night at the meeting. I could not concentrate my thoughts on the work of the service. I prayed and prayed so that I could follow the service, but to no avail. My thoughts were wandering, my mind riveted on our young folk at Mariah. There seemed a voice as if it said, 'You must go, you must go!'" — Evan Roberts in a letter to Mary Evan

Evan decided to delay his studies at the seminary and return to his hometown of Mariah to work with the young people in his city. When he arrived he learned that his pastor was having a church prayer meeting that night at his home church, Mariah Chapel. Evan boldly addressed his pastor asking permission to preach. His pastor agreed to allow him to preach, but told him that he could preach only after the prayer meeting was over. A meager group of seventeen people stayed behind to hear the word of the Lord from Evan. He preached that night about the coming revival that was to erupt in Wales. His sermon was the ground work for what would later become known as the four tenants of the Welsh Revival.

- You must confess any known sin
- Removal of everything doubtful in your life
- Entire commitment to the Spirit of God
- Public confession of Christ

It began in Mariah Chapel that night. Evan Roberts became the human instrument, the spark of revival to his nation that would set the dry wood burning. Spontaneous prayer and worship of God began to erupt in Evan's meetings. There was very little preaching, but worship, testimony and prayer were the main emphasis of the Holy Spirit. There were no hymnbooks used. They had learned the hymns in childhood. There was no robed choir, but every voice sang out. The fire of God could be felt not only in those present in the meetings, but it spilled out and into the nation of Wales and eventually the explosion would reach around the world.

Evan Roberts (1878 –1951)

A Fire, But Not on Your Terms

It's beautiful to see churches everywhere desire after revival. Many busy themselves praying for and singing about revival. They talk and preach sermons about the great revivals of the past and prophecy about the last great "end-time" revival yet to come.

Time and time again we've watched the Holy Spirit answer the prayers of churches as the trickles of an outpouring begin. We may be invited to a church or conference to be what Evan Roberts was to Mariah, fire starters. We bring with us Holy fire and the spirit of revival is poured out in great measure. And then, sadly, very soon church politics get involved or perhaps we get word from church leadership that the meetings are running a little too late. Maybe someone allows themselves to be offended and complain to the pastor and expect him to quickly make everything comfortable for them once again. My wife and I call this the "Revival on my terms syndrome." Churches desire revival fire as long as the fire starts and continue on their terms and within their timetable and guidelines, which is usually determined by the Sunday morning crowd instead of the prayer meeting crowd.

"I don't care how it [revival] comes, I just want it to come."
— Duncan Campbell

While revival begins with hunger it's fed by continually yielding to the Holy Spirit and to His purging and equipping fire. These two conditions, hunger and yielding, were met by Evan's and his young group. They had tapped into the kingdom mystery that so many Christians struggle to find. Some even say that the Welsh revival was the greatest revival since the book of Acts. And now, over a century later, we read their stories and view that time as religiously romantic and in some ways unattainable. But the conditions for revival haven't changed. They've always been the same, hunger and passion; along with a willingness to yield to the Spirit of God no matter how foolish one looks or feels.

Revival Worship is Essential

As a young boy my step-father would sometimes allow me tag along during hunting trips into the deep Montana woods. I remember how he would carefully build the campfire each night. First he'd place the thick, densest wood into a circle within the fire pit. Then he'd find dry, light kindling and lay in the inner circle where he wanted the source of the fire to burn. Lastly he'd find a handful of dried leaves and brush to ensure a quick burst of flame. His campfire building skills sure helped on those cold nights. Like my step-father had done when making his campfires, Evan Roberts also did when setting ablaze that small handful of seventeen young people. They became the kindling, the brush that lit quickly and spread fast. He placed them in the circle of passionate prayer and worship, knowing that all around was lukewarm Christians and stone-hard sinners who both needed a savior. The results were astounding.

"Then another angel, having a golden censer, came and stood at the altar. He was given much incense, that he should offer it with the prayers of all the saints upon the golden altar which was before the throne. And the smoke of the incense, with the prayers of the saints, ascended before God from the angel's hand. Then the angel took the censer, filled it with fire from the altar, and threw it to the earth. And there were noises, thundering's, lightning's, and an earthquake." (Revelation 8:3-5)

Revelation 8 refers to the incense and also to the prayers of the saints that were gathered by an angel. The incense is a beautiful picture of worship. Deep and passionate worship was an earmark of the Welsh revival. And just as the angel gathered up the prayers and threw them back to earth, the prayers and worship offered up in Wales in 1904 were also thrown back to earth causing spiritual earthquakes, thunder and the lightning's of God.

Revival worship is the one element that will propel any move of God and sustain it. It is the element that will cause an eruption of God's Spirit in any culture, in any town, in any nation, and in any situation. No matter how hard the "spiritual ground" is in your city, I guarantee the Christian folks in the next town over are saying the same thing. No matter how deep you might believe that the "satanic stronghold" is in your city, I guarantee that just over the city limit line they believe it's stronger there. But, what happened to Christians believing the word of God? Greater is HE that is in ME, than he that is in the world. [I John 4:4] If the Spirit of God lives within you then let Him show during worship. Show your passion, show your emotions. Let Him lead the worship for a change and watch the spirit of revival begin to trickle in; slowly at first and before you know the river of revival will be so deep that you cannot swim any longer and you lose control and let the river get inside of you. The worship that flowed during Evan's meetings were not bound by man because he believed God's word and understood that God inhabits the spiritual praises of His people.

Many preachers believe that their talented and amazing preaching is more than enough to draw all the lost and usher in a brilliant and lasting move of God. Don't misunderstand me. I believe in the importance of preaching and the importance of preaching truth…I'm a preacher. But pure, Spirit-led worship can take a person further faster into realms of God's glory and power than imaginable. Some of my most powerful experiences with the Holy Spirit took place during times of deep, passionate, Spirit-led worship and prayer.

Take a look at a typical Sunday morning service in any "seeker-sensitive" congregation and you're likely to find lingering in the atmosphere a sense of spectatorship. "Entertain and wow me," is the mentality of most attendees. And the leadership is all too pleased to keep the people happy, to give them what they want instead of what they need. (Sounds to me like a bad case of living in Laodicea.) Trust me friend, I've been around the church circuit. I've seen everything from concert style worship leaders singing secular, ungodly songs to folks chillin' out sipping on coffee and pounding down donuts. I've even seen Lazyboy recliners adorn the front of one church sanctuary. The stories I could tell you are endless and so is the apathy in these churches.

When we get out of our spectator mode and move away from our "entertain me" mentality then the Kingdom of God will crash with its powerful waves into our man-centered institutions. Then we'll begin to understand that our worship has become twisted and perverted. We'll be able to place the focus where it has always belonged, on Christ and on Him crucified; on the Father of Light, and on the precious Holy Spirit. The worship and prayers of God's people will usher the next move of God that has been prophesied time and time again that will shake planet Earth. The sooner we open our hearts to worshiping in Spirit and in Truth the sooner we can see what they saw and experience what they experienced in the revivals that you're reading about in this book.

"And the twenty-four elders who sat before God on their thrones fell on their faces and worshiped God, saying: "We give You thanks, O Lord God Almighty, The One who is and who was and who is to come, Because You have taken Your great power and reigned. The nations were angry, and Your wrath has come, And the time of the dead, that they should be judged, And that You should reward Your servants the prophets and the saints, And those who fear Your name, small and great, And should destroy those who destroy the earth." Then the temple of God was opened in heaven, and the ark of His covenant was seen in His temple. And there were lightning's, noises, thundering's, an earthquake, and great hail." (Revelation 11:16-19)

Spontaneous worship and prayer were earmarks of the 1904 Welch revival, and that, in some way, bothered many of the religious leaders. Their Pharisaical minds questioned how God could move night after night, drawing the lost to Christ, with just prayer and worship. But the power of the Holy Spirit wasn't limited to church meetings. Through the people the fire reached out into the streets of the city, into the country side, and beyond the shores of Wales. The conditions for revival were present and the wood was prepared. The spark had ignited in prayer and worship.

"It will not do for us to go to Heaven by ourselves. We must be on fire friends, for saving others. To be workers will draw heaven down and will draw others to heaven. Without a readiness to work, the Spirit of prayer will not come." — Evan Roberts

Unstoppable Fires

The Holy fire within these young people could not be quenched. Religion and tradition could not stop them from burning. The fire that consumed them was so transferable that it caught fire all around and prayer meetings were erupting like small infernos engulfing the entire nation of Wales from one village or township to the next. The fire was unstoppable. News of its force was heard of all over the world. In fact, word reached all the way to the burning hot revival taking place on Azusa Street in Los Angeles, California. Frank Bartleman, a journalist and holy preacher, corresponded in letter with Evan. In the last letter Evan wrote to Bartleman he stated, "I pray God to hear your prayer, to keep your faith strong, and to save California."

"The revival in South Wales is not of men, but of God. He has come very close to us. ... We are teaching... only the wonder and beauty of Christ's love. ... I am not the source of this revival, but only one agent among what is growing to be a multitude." — Evan Roberts (in a letter to Frank Bartleman) Azusa Street

27

CHAPTER 4
FIRE THAT COULD JUMP THE OCEAN

"Then you call on the name of your gods, and I will call on the name of the Lord; and the God who answers by fire, He is God."
(1 Kings 18:40)

What he said didn't surprise me, but it did frustrate me a bit. I sat across the table from one of my oldest friends who pastors an Assembly of God congregation in the United States. If I've heard it said once, I've heard it said a thousand times before from ministers, some well-intended and some not well-intended, who are desperately trying to either be spiritual or just sound radical. He said to me this, "Tom, I want revival so badly, but I just want to be sure that it's not us and it's all God." I understood what he was trying to say, but I couldn't disagree more with how it was stated. In his attempt to "give God all the glory" he had missed the mark completely. He was speaking from his theology and not from the word of God.

As an avid student of revival church history, I've read every book I can get my hands on about revivals of the past, not to mention over twenty-five years of study in God's word, which is packed with revival history from the beginning to the end. I could probably quote in my sleep dates, names, and the locations of revivals that you have never even heard about. Ask my wife, if we are traveling in a new town I will always stop to find out if there is a Christian bookstore just on the odd chance that it may be Charismatic and may carry revival books I've not yet read.

Quite honestly, in all my studies of great men and woman of God and of great and tremendous outpourings of renewals and revivals, I've never once read about how God did it without using men and women. That would be impossible. What is possible, however, is that an outpouring of revival is always ALL GOD and ALL MAN. That's possible – it's just how God designed it to be.

Evan Roberts understood this too. Evan prepared his heart in those early months, just prior to the revival, knowing that God needed a spark, a man, a deliverer, to ignite revival. There is and always has been a figurehead of every revival. They are the ones to carry the torch and lead the way. Does it always have to be led by a pastor? Certainly not. Look throughout history and you'll see many examples of men and women who were evangelists, missionaries, worship leaders, and even teachers like Charles Parham, Evan Roberts, Kathryn Kuhlman, Charles and John Wesley, Billy Sunday, Maria Woodworth-Etter, Billy Graham, and many, many more. Yet, John Kilpatrick, the pastor of the Pensacola, Florida Revival and Steve Gray the pastor of the Smithton Outpouring in Smithton, Missouri both led two of the most recent revival outpourings of our generation, as pastors.

Sadly, history tells us that leadership, or lack of leadership, would eventually be the downfall of the Welsh Revival. This came through a constant barrage of words from various church leaders placing doubt in Roberts mind regarding his ability and authority to lead the outpouring.

While God was preparing young Evan in Europe His Holy fire was in full blaze with Brother Charles Parham across the ocean in America, who was carrying and sharing the fire from Kansas to much of the United States. Word began to spread worldwide about what was happening and when Evan heard about God's goodness in the United States, his desire for the fire to reach into his nation only intensified. From 1901 to 1904 the fire was jumping the oceans of America and reaching other nations and people, including Wales.

On November 7, 1904 Mariah Chapel filled for a powerful prayer meeting that would last until the early morning hours of the following day. Filled to capacity the hungry were there to cry out to God for divine cleansing and to ask for Holy fire from Heaven. This was the famous prayer meeting when the Power of God rippled through those who had gathered and where Evan, being so burdened for the lost souls who would have to be "bent" on judgment day, he cried aloud the legendary prayer, "Bend us...bend us." This revival prayer became a staple prayer prayed frequently in the Welsh Revival, but most especially by Evan himself.

"If sinners be dammed, at least let them leap to Hell over our bodies. If they will perish, let them perish with our arms about their knees. Let no one GO there UNWARNED and UNPRAYED for."
— C. H. Spurgeon

In The Story of the Welsh Revival Roberts wrote:
"For a long, long time I was much troubled in my soul and my heart by thinking over the failure of Christianity. Oh! It seemed such a failure—such a failure—and I prayed and prayed, but nothing seemed to give me any relief. But one night, after I had been in great distress praying about this, I went to sleep, and at one o'clock in the morning suddenly I was waked up out of my sleep, and I found myself with unspeakable joy and awe in the very presence of the Almighty God. And for the space of four hours I was privileged to speak face to face with Him as a man speaks face to face with a friend. At five o'clock it seemed to me as if I again returned to earth."

Evan's heart had been torn with the lost condition of his country and further broken as he witnessed how the effects of lifeless religion had ruined the people's hunger for God. As he cried out to God he was amazed to learn how religion also broke the heart of God.

W.T. Stead wrote in his book, What I Saw In Wales: The Revival in the West:
"These people, all the people in a land like ours, are taught to death, preached to insensibility. They all know the essential truths. They know that they are not living as they ought to live, and no amount of teaching will add anything to that conviction...Revival is a rouser rather than a teacher."

By now the Revival in Wales was accelerating. The blazing inferno was touching the lives of believers and churches, and it was also touching the lives of the lost in an unprecedented craze. Taverns went empty and soon bankrupt, drunkenness was almost unfound any longer, and when someone tried to drink the mug of ale it would stick, supernaturally, to the bar, leaving the person unable to drink the brew. During the revival there was a dramatic drop in illegitimate pregnancies and people were living in Christian holiness unlike the nation had ever witnessed.

Evan Roberts

"There are different kinds of fire; there is false fire. No one knows this better than we do, but we are not such fools as to refuse good bank notes because there are false ones in circulation; and although we see here and there manifestations of what appears to us to be nothing more than mere earthly fire, we nonetheless prize and value, and seek for the genuine fire which comes from the altar of the Lord." — General William Booth

The Lost Found

The momentum of the Welsh revival was mounting and its flames were reaching the lost unlike they'd experienced in the United States under Charles Parham. It was gaining notoriety because of its emphasis on prayer and worship. And the fire was jumping oceans, denominations, doctrinal differences, genders, and race. Everyone, it seemed, was being affected by its flame, which appeared to be inextinguishable. It literally engulfed all who would embrace or come near to it. The eyewitnesses near Mariah Chapel would often see a flame flickering on top of the church steeple causing some to think that the church was literally burning. Some people testified that they would slip into the back of the churches to see what was going on, and although they started watching from the back of the church, within moments they were swept to the altar for salvation and soon they had become the ones worshiping and crying aloud for the fire to touch others.

For thirteen months this fire grew at a phenomenal rate and in that short period of strong worship and prayer they saw the entire country saved. Previous to this, all the church programs combined couldn't dent the hardness of society nor could it show any relevance to the lost condition of mankind. If programs were the Savior for your nation they would have already won the whole of the world to Christ. Church programs do little more than exploit and extract time, efforts, energy and money, leaving the people indifferent and untouched by the raw and real power of God. If extravagant, heartfelt, passionate worship and prayer did it in the book of Acts and in the country of Wales then it can and will do the same in your church, your town, and in your nation. Cannot God's power break the bands of wickedness and lifeless religion once again for us?

This aggressive flame grew to overwhelm the world in a little over a year's time. Many speculate as to why the fire ended as abruptly as it had started. One of the greatest influences on its conclusion was a woman named, Jessie Penn-Lewis, who inducing Evan to step down from leading the revival. Due to her unwise influence, Evan believed that by stepping away as its leader it would cause the fire to rage even higher and broader. Instead, his resignation quenched the fire. It was a firestorm in need of a leader. Unfortunately, Evan learned the hard lesson that God needed him for the revival as much as Evan needed God for the revival.

Evan Roberts remained a lover of revival throughout his life. He continued to live and pray for revival until his death in 1951 where he was buried on January 20th just behind Mariah Chapel, the place where it all began. Hundreds of people attended his memorial service to honor Evan for the life he had brought to the country of Wales and to the world. The last entry found written in his journal was one simple word, "ill."

What Can I Do To See Revival?

There are so many misguided myths of revival. Some preachers or teachers make the mistake of patterning their entire belief about revival from their study of just one or two revivals of the past. Some believe that by pitching a tent or constructing a building and placing a "revival" sign out front, that they've got it. But, I've found that most people overcomplicate revival. Revival is so easy. It's so basic, and yet so many so easily miss it. Revival begins in you. It's not something you must toil for, but it is something you must seek after. When the disciples told Jesus that they had toiled all the night to catch fish, He made it easy for them. He didn't overcomplicate it, but very simply He instructed them to cast their nets on the other side and what they gathered nearly sunk their vessel. Jesus made it easy.

"Not that I have already attained, or am already perfected; but I press on, that I may lay hold of that to which Christ Jesus has also laid hold of me. Brethren, I do not count myself to have apprehended; but one thing I do, forgetting those things which are behind and reaching forward to those things which are ahead."
– Paul the Apostle (Philippians 3:12-13)

Fathers of revival like, Charles Parham, Evan Roberts, William Seymour, and so many others found that there were basic, foundational things that they could do to attract the fire and maintain the fire. They were careful not to traditionalize these things and in so doing make them of no effect. Instead, with humble, hungry hearts they pursued the presence of God through:

1. Passionate, heart-felt worship
2. Consecration to the Holy Spirit [*What* He wants, *when* He wants it]
3. Accept and receive freely the grace of God – no more striving
4. Fasting of food for durations of time
5. A humble, teachable spirit
6. Constant, passionate prayer
7. A heart to serve others rather than be served

Revivals of the past have so many things to teach us about how to draw and preserve the fire of revival, but at the same time there are things we can learn to avoid too. These things are sure ways to destroy even the hope of revival. Any one of these will prohibit revival from starting, growing, spreading, and lasting:

1. Fakeness or a "need of nothing" Pharisee spirit
2. Criticism, pride, and stubbornness
3. Bitterness, back-biting, or bickering in the local body
4. False doctrine
5. Lack of grace and mercy
6. Apathy, laziness and selfishness

"Woe to you, scribes and Pharisees, hypocrites! For you travel land and sea to win one proselyte, and when he is won, you make him twice as much a son of hell as yourselves." (Matthew 23:15)

These are by no means exhaustive lists of "do's" and "don'ts," and I'm certain that there could not exist such a list. Revival is meant to be a perpetual state, where we allow the Holy fire that has touched us and set us free to continue to burn through us and to touch others in need. When the fire is turned up the weaknesses and impurities are exposed. As the fire burns within us it's only then that we learn about the religious Pharisee that may live in our heart. By yielding to the fire the pharisaical spirit is purged from our heart and we are molded to the Holy Spirit.

The story and the characters of the Welsh Revival are indeed intriguing and inspiring. Nothing had ever come over Wales with such incredible force and such incredible results. Total heathens were converted to Christ; drunkards and thieves were saved; confession of sin was common place; and lukewarm religion was made impossible. This tremendous outpouring was orchestrated by the Spirit of God. In just five weeks, twenty thousand people joined churches all over the country.

"Lord, dip me in the kerosene of your Spirit. Light me ablaze that I may burn for thee." – Charles Wesley

It's time again for a fire to jump an ocean to wherever you are right now. It's time for fire starters to ignite the next flame of God. My friend, I plead that you let the wonderful, unmatched Holy fire touch you just as it did with the prophet Isaiah. Let the coals of Heaven touch your lips, let the flames of God go into the deep places of your character and purify you.

I most sincerely implore you to let the fire of God begin to bubble up on the inside of you right where you sit this very moment. Let the hunger grow until there is nothing more than can satisfy the pangs except for more of His Holy fire.

Lord I groan, Lord I kneel
I'm crying out for something real
Cause I know deep in my soul
There must be more

Lord I'm tired, yes I'm weak
I need Your power to work in me
But I can't let go, I keep hanging on
There must be more
There must be more
There must be more

River flow, fire burn
River flow, fire burn

Holy Spirit breathe on me
Holy Spirit breathe on me

David Ruis
There Must Be More
Mercy Publishing; Vineyard Worship 1994

CHAPTER 5
IT ONLY TAKES A SPARK
TO GET A FIRE BURNING

The best tool for propelling any revival is heartfelt revival worship. It is the kind of worship that God responds to and loves. Heartfelt revival worship takes place when you worship God with hunger and mean it with all your heart. It is a journey, an experience, a dance. Heartfelt revival worship happens as we bow our hearts motives and consciously surrender everything to Him—it's allowing Him to become the Guest of Honor, the Center of it all.

"I said: 'Woe is me, for I am undone! Because I am a man of unclean lips, and I dwell in the midst of a people of unclean lips; For my eyes have seen the King, The Lord of hosts.' Then one of the seraphim flew to me, having in his hand a live coal, which he had taken with the tongs from the altar. And he touched my mouth with it..." (Isaiah 6:5-7)

As a kid I remember how I loved to sit my dad's lap on Saturday afternoons and watch the Minnesota Twins play baseball. And there were the rare, very rare, occasions we actually got to visit the Metrodome and watch the boys in blue up close – a hotdog in one hand, of course my catcher mitt in the other. Summer days were sometimes spent with dad teaching me how to hit a baseball. "Keep your eye on the ball," he would say over and over again. With dad's coaching I soon became the best hitter on our unofficial neighborhood kid's league and the envy of every teammate. In the simple game of baseball my father had taught me a valuable life lesson – to keep my eye on the ball.

Diversion and distraction keep people from obtaining their dreams and making their goals become reality. Sometimes it happens in their education, or their career, or even their marriage. But some of the greatest innovators and leaders in our lifetime, and all throughout history, are those who refused to be distracted. One such man was William Seymour. Brother Seymour, a black American, was born in May 1870 in Louisiana to parents who were former slaves. He was a humble man born before his time and he grew up to be the man that led revival, which according to some, was one of the "greatest revivals since the book of Acts."

There is no argument that Brother Seymour was one of the most humble men of God. His personality wasn't demanding or domineering, like that of Charles Parham, and he was not an introvert like Evan Roberts. But while Brother Seymour may have seemed an unlikely candidate in the eyes of man he was the right fit for God's choosing. Seymour willingly and humbly took the flack and foolishness from the religious world, but was never prone to cower away from bringing correction where and when it was needed. A godly man of the highest of moral standards, Seymour never seemed to wrestle with the usual trappings that have shipwrecked so many other great men and women of God.

Seymour – The Least Likely

After the Civil War in the United States President Lincoln's address of freedom for all Americans may have been heard by all, yet it wasn't heeded by all. Racism and oppression to the black community was severe in Louisiana during this time. With very little possessions, Seymour ventured to the North where he could receive a better education and employment opportunities. He eventually found himself in Indianapolis, Indiana, where he received Christ salvation and joined the Church of God Reformation movement, a conservative holiness group. There he was "sanctified" and called to be a minister.

In 1902, Seymour moved to Cincinnati, Ohio. While there he caught the near fatal disease, smallpox. Hundreds were dying all around him. Although he lived through the disease, its severity left him partially blind in one eye and badly scarred on one side of his face. To mask the grotesque scar Seymour grew a beard to cover the disfigurement.

William Seymour (1870 – 1922)

During the years of 1901 – 1905, Charles Parham's group made their journey further South traveling originally from Topeka, Kansas to Kansas City, Kansas and then onto Tulsa and Oklahoma City, Oklahoma. From there they traveled to northern Texas and finally ended in Houston, Texas where a Holy Spirit collision with destiny awaited them. In Houston, Texas, Parham advertised the bible school, as well as the baptism of the Holy Spirit. A handful of students joined him, including one man whose hunger for the Holy Spirit surprised even Parham. It was William Seymour. Seymour would later tell the story of how during that time the Holy Spirit asked him to pray more daily than he had ever prayed before. He went from praying two hours a day to praying four hours and then to praying eight hours each day. This incredible hunger was a divine set-up for him to collide with the fire carried by the Parham group. All it would take was a little spark to start a burning fire within in this man who would later be dubbed, "Papa Seymour" or "Daddy Seymour."

Unlike the freedom every American enjoys today, there were segregation laws in place during this time called, Jim Crow Laws. These ungodly laws, which existed from 1876 – 1965, prohibited black men and women from congregating alongside white men and women, which caused a hindrance for Seymour when joining the school with the other students who were white. To resolve this impediment, the bible school would leave a doorway open in the hall allowing Seymour to attend the school classes by listening through the doorway of the classroom. Rather than rising up in offense, which would have been understandable, Seymour refused to live in a state of insult. Instead, he became a sponge, soaking up the Anointing that flowed from the schoolroom.

Seymour became so acquainted with the revelation of the baptism of the Spirit that he would teach it in the black congregation meetings in Houston, just as Parham did among the whites. The two became friends and ministered frequently together, but in different congregations. Throughout this time, Seymour did not yet speak in other tongues, but he taught it as truth while the presence of God roared through those Houston meetings.

It was in one of those Houston meetings that a woman, hungry for the power of God, was in attendance. As she sat listening to his simple, calm, unemotional teaching she was convinced that he would be wonderful for a congregation in Los Angeles, California. When she returned to the small Holiness church in Los Angeles, she called Brother Seymour to come work and minister as their pastor. The churches current pastor, Julia Hutchinson, agreed and Seymour began arrangements for their California move to take over this pastorate.

"A revival almost always begins among the laity. The ecclesiastical leaders seldom welcome reformation. History repeats itself. The present leaders are too comfortably situated as a rule to desire innovation that might require sacrifice on their part. And God's fire only falls on sacrifice. An empty altar receives no fire!" — Frank Bartleman

Kicked Out of Church for the Fire

William Seymour arrived in southern California by train and after being confined to his small traveling quarters for days the hunger within him was like a caged tiger. He couldn't wait to preach about the revelations of God's word. It was his first meeting as the pastor and he preached from Acts 2:1-4. He boldly shared the baptism of the Holy Spirit and some of the manifestations of an infilling, including speaking in tongues. The meeting ended and Seymour left the building, but much to his amazement when he returned to the church the next day the doors were padlocked shut. Clearly he was not welcomed back. Seymour had just relocated his entire family, life, and ministry across the country. But still, he was not devastated; after all, he was kicked out for the sake of Holy fire.

What Seymour experienced that day was not uncommon and still is not uncommon. Revival history tells us that as far back as in the Acts of the early church, Paul the Apostle was getting kicked out, stoned, and even banished from towns because he preached the truth with Holy fire. And still Paul went on preaching and setting people free with power and the Anointing; not to mention writing two-thirds of the entire New Testament. The great revivalist, Charles Wesley, was kicked out of his own father's church when he taught about revival. As Wesley exited the church he walked straight out to the graveyard just outside the church building, climbed atop his father's gravestone, and preached all the louder until all the church people came outside to hear him burn with Holy fire.

I can remember a time when this happened to me and my wife, Susie. We'd been invited to travel to another part of the country some two-thousand miles away to preach on revival. The church had advertised the "revival" meetings in the local paper and had invited other church congregations to join in the weeks meetings. We'd done a lot of advertising ourselves and we were expecting several hundred visitors to join this congregation. The pastor phoned our office about a week before the meetings were to begin in a state of panic because he said that so many people had been calling the church office for directions and he was very concerned that there wouldn't be adequate seating in the 300 seat sanctuary. With panic in his voice he explained that it was now far too late to rent a larger building anywhere in his small city. The pastor was beside himself with anxiety and stress. I quickly calmed him down and reminded him that this "problem" was something we'd prayed to have happen and that clearly God was up to something and that we should go ahead and continue with the week of meetings. I assured him that this was a sure sign of hunger in the hearts of God's people and to let the people come.

On the first night of meetings the place was packed. Every seat was filled and people were seated on the floor of the isles and in the back of the sanctuary. Some resorted to perching up into the window sills as God's word and power swept through the church. As I preached I felt the Holy Spirit fire so tangibly. I preached the word of the Lord that night and people were weeping and rushing to find a place at the altar. Others were standing with their hands lifted toward heaven receiving with open arms. God was busy healing broken bones and diseases well before either Susie or I had a chance to pray for them. Clearly God was setting them free of the doctrines of man. The success of any true minister is seeing the faces of people as they encounter our powerful God. We stayed to pray for everyone in the building that night. It was late by the time we gathered our things to leave the sanctuary. I looked to my wife and told her what a great week we had ahead of us here among these hungry people.

Unfortunately, the leadership of the church didn't agree. By the time we reached the lobby of the church we were met by a sort of "lynch mob" formed of church leaders and board members, and in the middle of the group stood the pastor. Sticking his boney finger in my nose he summonsed us to his office. During this "sit-down" I held my tongue as a whirlwind of their "denominational beliefs" came shooting from their mouths. It was only moments before that I had revealed to them what God's beliefs were using Bible scriptures, the words of Jesus, Himself. How could it be my fault that their denominational beliefs and God's beliefs didn't match? I'd like to say that when he sat us down in his office that we spoke together as Christian brothers, full of grace, sharing with one another our disagreements, but what we heard isn't worth repeating to you, so I won't. Needless to say, we were told that we had five minutes to gather our belongings and leave the church. And as many revivalists before us had done, we walked out of the church doors and shook off the dust.

You see, religion doesn't care how precious the fruit, nor is it concerned with the truth of God's word. Religion's only concern is about what man-made tradition says. It was much the same when Seymour found himself at a loss, because the people had been so obviously blessed by the truths he had preached.

44

This may have set Seymour back a bit, but it certainly didn't stop him. Just as Parham had done during his visit to Zion, Illinois, Seymour took the meetings and the fire into someone's home. Richard and Ruth Asberry opened their house to Seymour, to the hungry people, and most importantly to the fire. Their home was the famous 214 North Bonnie Brae Street.

214 North Bonnie Brae Street

In the Asberry home, gathered a group of people from many different nationalities - black, white, Hispanic, it didn't matter. They all assemble together there. At that time Seymour had been staying in the home of Mr. Edward Lee and it was Mr. Lee who would be the first to break out aloud speaking in other tongues on the night of April 9, 1906. After Mr. Lee spoke in tongues it began to happen in a domino effect and one by one they each exploded into other tongues. Once again, a fire that started as a little spark would soon ignite into a blazing inferno.

Soon other strange manifestations of the Spirit began to take place among the group. Some would suddenly fall onto the floor seemingly struck by the power of God. One of his neighbors had joined the meetings; Jennie Evan Moore, who supernaturally began to play the piano, which was something she did not have the ability to do before she experienced the outpouring of the Spirit. As this continuous outflow of the Spirit occurred, many hundreds of people began to congregate to this unlikely place until there were so many gathered into the streets that Seymour would to have to perch himself up on the porch of the Bonnie Brae house to preach about the fire.

Three days into this incredible outpouring Seymour's prayers had been answered and he too was baptized in the Holy Spirit and spoke in tongues for the first time.

Seymour, it seemed, had been kicked out of favor with leaders of the church and kicked into favor with almighty God. When they locked him out of the church he was about to be locked into revival history as the man, who against all odds, burned hot with the fire of God. From those meetings, Seymour founded the Apostolic Faith Mission.

More Signs and Wonders

There was no lack in the realm of the supernatural at Azusa Street. Men and woman were regularly experiencing supernatural visions and dreams and it wasn't limited to the members of Apostolic Faith Mission. Visitors who had traveled from all over the world frequently testified of experiencing the same phenomenon. Spiritual dreams and visions were so common that they were happening even among people who were yet unsaved, pointing them in the direction of Christ Jesus. Some would have open visions of Jesus, and other of angels.

"And they were all amazed, and they glorified God, and were filled with [holy] fear, saying, 'we have seen strange things today'." (Luke 5:26)

Trances were often experienced and described as having happened after people had fallen to the floor by the power of the Spirit. They would lay there motionless, sometimes for hours. Some even experience trances as they stood during the service, in a frozen like state for long durations of time without blinking or appearing to sweat. Trances, dreams, and visions may be strange to you, and they may be uncommon in your church or ministry, but these supernatural happenings were the promise that the prophet Joel prophesied and then took place in Acts 2 when Pentecost had come. Supernatural signs point us to Jesus and to the Kingdom of God while the

Heavenly wonders make us wonder upon the greatness and vastness of our Heavenly Father that has come to dwell among us, mere men and women.

Susie and I have seen this many, many times in our ministry over the years. Instead of trying to reason out what we don't understand, like the Pharisees do, we simply believe that if the Bible says we should have it then we should have it, and if we don't have it then we need to get it, because it's good and it's godly. Many people who've attended our meetings have had experiences with supernatural dreams, visions and even trances. Some have been very young children. I remember when an eight year old girl in Southern Texas went into a spiritual trance for over four hours. When she came to herself she couldn't stop speaking in another tongue. She shared later with her parents and us how she was with Jesus and together they ran through a large and beautiful field of flowers playing "tag-you're-it." It makes me weep when I think back on how she described Him, so gentle, so personal, so hers.

One of the most well-known supernatural wonders of the Azusa Street revival were the eyewitness testimonies of the flames of fire coming from the rooftop of the old warehouse that was home to the Apostolic Faith Mission church. In fact, that phenomenon happened so regularly that it's recorded that the Los Angeles fire department was dispatched 33 times to put out the fire. Each time the firefighters would arrive they found no natural fire burning, not even the odor of smoke.

The Strengths of William Seymour

Some may have mistaken his humility for insecurity, but William Seymour was anything but insecure. I've met few Christian leaders who are confident enough in who they are and in their own gift and ministry calling that they are to be free to build and release others into their gifts and ministry callings. In fact, it's my opinion that it was one of the most lacking characteristics to come out of most of the revivals and outpourings in the 1990s. Sadly, some church leaders minister out of a poverty mentality when it comes to their invested treasure in people. Because of fear, or a need to control, they tighten their grip on people, using whatever means necessary, such as manipulation, control, and fear; instead of sowing and releasing them into the harvest fields, and in turn, believe God for a better return on their investment into the Kingdom.

"Give me one hundred preachers who fear nothing but sin and desire nothing but God, and I care not whether they be clergymen or laymen, they alone will shake the gates of hell and set up the Kingdom of Heaven upon earth." — Leonard Ravenhill

Seymour had the amazing, but rare, ability to patiently and gracefully equip the people and also release the people into their calling out in the mission harvest field. Pointing people into their destinies, he clearly supported their hunger to give the fire away, even, and most especially, if it meant they would leave his church and minister the fire somewhere else throughout the world. Seymour realized revival as a great tool of empowerment for the people. He would encourage them to host their very own revival services with the purpose to see the fire spread. Often Seymour would bless them by collecting an offering for them and then he would advertise their ministry meetings in the Apostolic Faith Newspaper, harboring no agenda except to see the expansion of God's Spirit among men.

There is an old song that goes "It only takes a spark to get a fire going. And soon all those around, can warm up in its glowing." This worship song from years gone by rings in my heart each time I reflect on Brother Seymour and upon his place in revival history. Seymour's heart was to reach beyond those of his own skin color or national status. Instead he wanted everyone affected and infected with the fire of the Holy Spirit.

Seymour was sensitive and open to allowing the Holy Spirit to flow freely about his ministry, yet he was never afraid to bring correction to man during a service. Allowing his services to become a "free-for-all" didn't interest him. If a guest minister arrived to preach and Seymour didn't agree with him on a doctrinal level he would assure him or her that it wasn't to be preached again under his ministry. If another minister "missed the flow" of the Holy Spirit he would gently, but firmly, guide him back. When the great revivalist, Charles Parham, preached the ungodly traditions of racial division at Azusa Street, Seymour willingly rebuked his former teacher.

One of the most admired strengths of Seymour was his eagerness to always give both, praise and correction, when called for, to those under his leadership, never insisting on a need to control anyone by withholding either virtue.

The Essential Ingredients

It was common for the outpouring meetings to have a-cappella singing and occasionally an instrument or two, but one thing they never had was an agenda, besides God. Much like what happened during the outpouring revival meetings in Wales, there were always testimonies, singing and worship, and heart felt prayer. Spontaneous was the word best used to describe what God did in those early days of the revival.

1 Corinthians 14:15 says, "I will pray, I will sing..." Isn't this a great picture of revival worship and revival prayer? This same pattern is marked throughout the book of Acts in the early Church. The church at Corinth understood the power of praying and worship because of Paul's words, which were etched into their hearts by the Holy Spirit. Worship and prayer must be integral parts of our churches today if we are to ask and seek after revival. Through heartfelt worship and prayer, Seymour led the revival into the fire of God. It was because of these essential ingredients that the revival continued to grow, holding three services per daily for many years.

"Many of us are living for nothing else. A volume of believing prayer is ascending to the throne night and day. Los Angeles, Southern California, and the whole continent shall surely find itself before long in the throes of a mighty revival, by the Spirit and power of God. – Way of Faith, Nov 16, 1905." — Frank Bartleman

These men, Charles Parham, Evan Roberts, and William Seymour, along their groups were keys to the charismatic, manifestations of Holy Spirit freedom, we so liberally enjoy today. They broke open so that we, generations later, could break through. They endured the worst of criticism, ridicule and mockery, from of the majority religious leaders of their day. There are stories of rotten tomatoes and eggs that were thrown at them as they walked in town. It was common for businessmen to deny doing business with them and instead closed down the store when they would arrive. Maybe you can agree with me that today, we Pentecostal Christians, have it quite easy in comparison. We have such a rich treasure of what can so easily be taken for granted. I am so thankful for these brave and courageous pioneers who refused to be made silent; who raged on with the inner passion to further establish the kingdom of Heaven among men.

"The hand of the Lord was upon me, and he brought me out by the Spirit of the Lord and set me in the middle of a valley; it was full of bones... Then he said to me, "Prophesy to the breath; prophesy, son of man, and say to it, 'This is what the Sovereign Lord says: Come from the four winds, O breath, and breathe into these slain, that they may live.'" So I prophesied as he commanded me, and breath entered them; they came to life and stood up on their feet--a vast army" (Ezekiel 37:1-10 emphases added).

CHAPTER 6
FEEDING THE FIRE

From the Asberry's home on Bonnie Brae Street, Seymour and his hungry herd moved the daily meetings into an abandoned warehouse building at 312 Azusa Street in Los Angeles, California, which had been used as a livery stable. They rented the rough, rustic building and established the Apostolic Faith Mission.

The first meeting took place on the night before Easter Sunday, Saturday April 14, 1906 and little did they know what the future would hold. About a hundred people gathered that night and they were hungry for the fire. Many nationalities were assembled including men and women of different skin color. It is said that through the Holy Spirit they became color blind. They sat, side by side, on old wooden boards. Sawdust covered the hard wood floors. It was dirty, filthy by most standards. No, it wasn't a conventional church to say the least. A shoebox was used as a make-shift pulpit and yet none of it seemed to stand in the way of the Holy Spirit.

Azusa Street revival (Apostolic Faith Gospel Mission)

The following morning was Easter Sunday. The hungry group congregated in their newly established, but dingy church building. Sister Moore rose that morning to share with so many others of her testimony about how she too had received the Holy Spirit and even spoke in other tongues. She prophesied that morning about three visions she had and even predict a soon coming calamity. It was only three days later that the largest earthquake hit the United States and the 1906 San Francisco Fire would engulf the city leaving massive devastation.

Lightning, Fire, and Earthquakes, Oh My!

The Azusa Street revival erupted in 1906. Ironically, on January 31 of the same year, one of the largest earthquakes on record (8.2 on the Richter scale) would strike just off the coast of Ecuador. More ironically, on April 18th of the same year another earthquake would strike San Francisco, California (7.8 on the Richter scale), not far from Los Angeles, which was the biggest earthquake in United States history. The 1906 San Francisco Earthquake caused the largest and most devastating fire ever to batter an American city and was eventually dubbed, "The 1906 San Francisco Fire." No, I don't believe that these disasters are supernatural and that God is setting off earthquakes or starting fires to show off His power, nor to show that He wants to destroy the earth. Yet, I do wonder if these natural disasters are the very earth itself groaning for the revealing of God's sons and daughters who are equipped with the manifested Spirit of God to change the world.

It happened at the crucifixion. Immediately after Jesus was crucified the Bible speaks of a massive earthquake that struck and graves were emptied. Later on, we learn that when Jesus was raised from the dead there was an earthquake too. Remember when Paul and Silas prayed and sang praises to God while in the jail in Acts 16? The Bible says that the earthquake was so violent that it even released the chains from every prisoner. Many biblical revivals and important events seemed to be marked with an earthquake; and while I wouldn't make a doctrine out of this, I do find it very interesting.

The Journalist Frank Bartleman

From the beginning of the outpouring, people were drawn. Frank Bartleman was one such person. A journalist by trade, Bartleman would later become known as a nationally recognized evangelist. Perhaps Bartleman is most well-known today for chronicling the Azusa Revival and other revival happenings around the world. He

52

knew the power of the media, the written word and its ability to catapult the outpouring worldwide.

Frank Bartleman had a unique ability to capture people with his writings, moving them either to action or to hunger. In fact, he became the editor of the Azusa Street revival newspaper, The Apostolic Faith Newspaper. In the newspaper were transcriptions of Seymour's sermons along with news of the meetings and the many missionaries that were sent forth from the revival. The circulation reached well over 50,000. After the earthquakes of 1906 and "The 1906 San Francisco Fire," Bartleman published a Pentecostal tract about them. Thousands of the tracts, filled with end-time prophecies, were widely distributed.

Besides Brother Seymour, Bartleman was the strongest voice for the Azusa Street and for the ministry of Brother William Seymour. He had the heart for ministry from beginning to end, and he passionately embraced the Holy fire.

"The very truths that gave birth to the Pentecostal movement are today generally rejected as too strong." — Frank Bartleman

Packed Into This Small Building

The building was a simple wood frame structure that stood forty feet by sixty feet in size. Seymour would later use the upstairs apartment as his family residence because, it is said that he wanted to be as close as possible to what God was doing in each service. Because each time they met together it was the service of the Holy Spirit, every service was different and there was no specific "order of service." Seymour explained, "The scriptures tell us that the wind blows where it wills and we just follow the wind." Sometimes they would pray for the sick and witness incredible miracles and other times there was a holy silence that lasted for hours until a busting forth as they sang together in English or in tongues. Offerings were never collected by passing the plate, but instead Seymour placed a receptacle at the door to receive the love offerings from the people. The majority of the funds collected would be given away to the poor and needy or to missionaries in other parts of the world.

Brother Seymour positioned the pulpit in the middle of the room so that all could see and so that there would be plenty of room to receive from the Holy Spirit in healing, salvation or whatever it was that each seeker had come hungry to receive.

Outwardly the Apostolic Faith Mission was nothing special to gaze upon, but inwardly it was decorated with the finest that heaven had to offer. It was very common that people were slain in the Spirit or would fall down under the power of God for hours and many of them would have open visions. Services would swell from 300 to over 800. Once as many as 1,500 attended one service even though the building could only hold 400 seated with another 500 standing. That left over 600 people to stand outside during one of the hottest summers in Los Angeles history with no air-conditioning.

Numerical Growth, It Adds Up

Numerical growth is a byproduct of any true biblical and historical revival. In the case of Azusa Street, within a month, people were flooding into the church to see what God was doing. Both laypeople and ministers of all denominations and backgrounds came to the fire. The Pharisees who couldn't accept it showed up too. And just like natural burning fire attracts the moths, charlatans also would arrive, trying desperately to get their hands on a piece of the attraction. How amazing it is for our generation to see that without the internet, television, or much of our modern media, the Holy Spirit drew people worldwide to the California street called Azusa.

Los Angeles newspaper headlines April 18, 1906

Although Seymour had a timid personality, and by his own admission was more of a teacher than a preacher, when the Spirit would fall upon him he would suddenly become energized and greatly emotional. He would jump and run the aisles shouting the joy. But, in all that he did, he always allowed the Sprit to move freely, many times literally burying his head in the pulpit crate to cut off from the hysterics going on around him. Some would be weeping at the altar and others laughing in the Spirit and all the while Seymour just wanted to pray and inquire of the Lord as to what to do next.

Azusa Street Guests – Supporters and Opponents

Charles Parham would enter the scene of Azusa Street and cross paths with William Seymour one more time, but this time the former teacher would become the student, which proved to be very difficult for Parham's ego. In October of 1906, just six months after the fire had erupted on Azusa Street, Seymour invited Parham to preach on the baptism in the Spirit.

When Parham arrived he found it extremely difficult to overcome his traditional upbringing. To see the blacks and whites worshiping together, seated side by side, laughing together, singing together, weeping together, proved all too much for him despite the evidence of God's holy presence. He quickly mocked the liberality of the group and out of his soul, rather than out of his spirit, he shamed the people by telling them that God was displeased. But it was too late; they'd witnessed for themselves God's overwhelming approval through His handiwork amongst them. Parham was quickly asked to step down and leave - this way of thinking was not welcomed in the revival. It was a sad ending to their relationship, which had begun in the spirit of love and hunger. It was Parham's deep seeded insecurities that prevailed over his hunger, and in retaliation Parham soon formed a church nearby. It quickly failed due to a lack of unity.

Although many outside influences tried to corner him into separating the people, Seymour refused. It wasn't in his character or in his mindset to fuss and fight about doctrines and traditional racial tensions. His hunger won out over the insecurities and bigotry of others and all he wanted to do was see this outpouring propelled and launched to reach as many as possible.

Eventually the revival meetings were going seven days a week, with three meetings each day. This lasted for just over three years. It was common to hear people weeping and tarrying for the Spirit all night long for days at a time. Their tears soaked that sawdust covered floors and heaven acted, pouring out a mighty portion upon the hungry.

Like Charles Parham, the Spirit of God drew other well-known ministers, pastors, evangelists, and leaders from other movements. They all traveled to this humble place where God was visiting. When the revival had ended Frank Bartleman cried, "I'd give fifty years of my life just to have three more months of the Azusa Street Revival." Like Bartleman, I too have experienced revival in my own life and I know that once you've stood in the middle of the fire you just can't stand the smell of smoke.

There Must Be More

As I shared with you earlier, I was born again at the young age of sixteen in my western Minnesota town. This was a dramatic time in my life and I was instantly encouraged to receive the baptism of the Spirit and to speak in other tongues. I knew inside that there was more in God than the little that I'd experienced. Four months after my conversion I spoke in tongues in the first Spirit-filled church I'd ever attended. In order to get there I had to drive over a hundred miles in one direction. It was January in 1983. January in Minnesota is not the time of year to drive a hundred miles anywhere at night, especially in a car only a teenager would be agreeable to drive. Once I arrived to the church I could feel something special. The Spirit spun the congregation of 1,000 people like a cyclone. Given the invitation, I raced forward to receive the manifestation of tongues and be baptized in the Spirit of God. I couldn't contain my emotions and within seconds I erupted aloud speaking in tongues and crying. I knew instantly when I received the Spirit that there was a calling upon my life for the ministry. I knew that very night that with one touch of Holy fire so set my destiny in God.

"The depth of a revival will be determined exactly by the depth of the spirit of repentance." — Frank Bartleman

Mailing Lists Stolen

As Seymour was busy training up leaders from among his group to help him preach, minister to the sick, lay hands on the people and even work the altars, something sinister was stirring within his immediate staff and Seymour was unaware. Dissention and undermining had begun with his secretary, Clara Lum, and one of his leaders in the ministry who was also the editor of the Apostolic Faith Newspaper, Sister Florence Crawford. She slowly began to plant small seeds, unsuspecting at first, of discord in her articles which were being circulated to Seymour's entire mailing list. Those who read the paper began to sense the internal problems arising at the revival.

Ultimately Clara Lum and Sister Crawford devised a scheme to steal away the newspaper mailing list in an effort to leave with it and eventually use it to promote their own ministry. Their plot was successful. Clara and Sister Crawford moved to Portland, Oregon taking along with them the mailing list. Sadly, their sabotage led to the undoing of the revival.

Seymour Sees the End

The revival lasted for over three years. Its demise was attributed to leadership who didn't share Seymour's heart for the revival. After the crowds had long left him and the financial resources along with them, Seymour was still unmoved and refused to be discouraged. Seymour didn't just lead the revival, he was the revival and he loved and embraced it to the very end.

Last Words of His Fire

People's last words can carry great value and meaning. In Seymour's simple way he uttered his last words, "I love my Jesus so." Brother Seymour was buried in Los Angeles' Evergreen Cemetery. Those that supported him to the end of his life engraved on his tombstone, "Our Pastor." The loss to the Pentecostal world and to Christianity in general was great the day he joined in the cloud.

Present at his funeral were his family members and a few close friends from both his ministry and his life. Frank Bartleman wept.

CHAPTER 7
SHARE THE FIRE

From 1900 to 1910 the world experienced a powerful awakening. Such an awakening had not been experienced since the days following the crucifixion of Jesus, when the Anointing of Holy fire invaded the upper room and the men and women waiting for Him that day. The Holy Spirit was eager to, at last, occupy the minds and bodies of men and women, and once again set planet Earth back on its correct course of Godly destiny.

The Topeka Revival, the Welsh Revival, and the Azusa Street Revival, all experienced the fire of God during this period of world history. All three of these revivals were birthed out of a man's passionate pursuit of "the more" that is found only in the fire of God. All three of these revivals blessed the people of their nation, and beyond its borders. All three of these revivals were overwhelmed with supernatural visitations of signs, wonders and miracles. But the most impacting attribute of all three was their holy fervor to share the fire among the nations.

These radical revivalists were willing to equip their people with Holy fire and release them into the ministry fields. Growing up on a farm I can remember that each night the sheep would be herded from the pasture into a small fenced pen. Although this was done for the good of each of them within the group, they couldn't understand that. Once they were all placed inside of the pen they would be fed and given sheltered rest for the night, but first thing in the morning they were ready for release. I enjoyed watching the sheep frolic and jump up and down, sometimes landing on top of each other with anticipation and excitement as my grandfather would open the gate each morning. This is a lot like the believer who has been penned up in the throes of revivals fire. He's been placed their because of the grace of the Father in order to find rest from religion and tradition, and to be fed to fullness with the consuming flames of Holy fire. Now, can you image the injustice of forcing him to remain inside his locked up confines for the sake of an insecure shepherd, afraid to lose him if he lets him free?

"God is the God of revival, but man is the human agent through whom revival is possible." — Duncan Campbell, The Lewis Awakening

Win the Lost at Any Cost

If a revival has manifestations, signs, and wonders, but is not saving souls, then the fire of revival will eventually fade away leaving nothing except man-centered traditions and a golden-calf religion. The people affected by the fire must be released to share the fire. Multi-media outlets were not called to win the lost. Christian television, no matter how resourceful, wasn't handed the great commission. The Ark of God's presence was supposed to be carried upon the shoulders of men and never intended to be carried on a cart of oxen. The same thing is true today. The Ark, the place of safety and refuge, Holy fire, is to rest upon the shoulders of men and women and be carried out into the city streets, to the country sides, to the gutters and to high-society.

"I have but one passion: It is He, it is He alone. The world is the field and the field is the world; and henceforth that country shall be my home where I can be most used in winning souls for Christ." — Count Nicolaus Ludwn Zinzendorf

Someone loved you enough to share Christ with you. I believe that because you are reading this book you are probably hungry for more Holy fire. Someone was selfless the day they shared with you about the Grace and Life that was waiting for you within the Ark of Salvation. Thanks be to God for their obedience and for their deep passionate commitment to share the Holy fire with you. The day they opened their mouth, they weren't as much concerned about their reputation, as they were more deeply concerned for the condition of your soul. Would to God that more Holy Spirit believers would take more seriously their call and their divine command to win the lost at any cost.

"Could a mariner sit idle if he heard the drowning cry?
Could a doctor sit in comfort and let his patients die?
Could a fireman sit idle, let me burn and give no hand?
Can you sit at ease in Zion with the world around you DAMNED?"
— Leonard Ravenhill

As believers we must choose to learn from trailblazers like Charles Parham, Evan Roberts, and William Seymour. These men ignited a fire that is still burning within the hearts of Pentecostal, Charismatic believers. Their fire in unquenchable and it's contagious – it's Holy fire and it lives inside of you. Like them, you too can stoke the embers, taking revival any place and at any time. Give some of it away and you'll learn how quickly more comes back to you. It's supernatural. It defies logic and that's why the critics cannot take part. Choose today to join in with the great cloud of witnesses that surrounds you, cheering you on to catch more of the fire, to run with the fire, and above all, to share the fire.

The Talking Stones from 1900-1910

Men like Seymour, Parham, and Roberts, have moved on and into the realm of heaven, leaving behind them their many works that speak to us as spiritual stones. Like in Joshua 4:1-6, we look upon these stones to observe, admire, embrace, and learn from what God did in their lives. Get hungry to do what these men did and even more. Stand on their shoulders and take the same Holy fire to greater lengths. The scripture tells us that everything pertaining to life and godliness has already been given to you (2 Peter 1:3). You've been equipped, my friend. Allow the lives and ministries of these men to encourage and charge you forward and speak to your heart of hunger, passion, prayer, worship, souls and sacrifice.

The time for revival is NOW. The time for the lost to come to Jesus is NOW. The time for the Holy fire to fall is NOW. And the place for it to happen is in YOU. Revival is just that easy.

"The marvelous wave of God came over the country from 1900 to 1906 when hundreds of thousands were baptized in the Holy Ghost and spoke in tongues." — John G. Lake

61

(You may download free evangelism materials from our website at: www.SHAREtheFIRE.org)

BIBLIOGRAPHY

Synon, Vinson The Century of the Holy Spirit

Borlase, Craig William Seymour a biography

Parham, Charles F. A Voice Crying in the Wilderness. Baxter Springs, Kan.: Apostolic Faith Bible College; originally published in 1902; 2d ed. in 1910.

The Everlasting Gospel. Baxter Springs, Kan.: Apostolic Faith Bible College, 1911.

Parham, Robert L., comp. Selected Sermons of the Late Charles F. Parham, Sarah E. Parham. Baxter Springs, Kan.: Apostolic Faith Bible College, 1941.

Parham, Sarah E. The Life of Charles F. Parham, Founder of the Apostolic Faith Movement. Baxter Springs, Kan.: Apostolic Faith Bible College, 1930.

http://www.stonesfolly.com

Goff, James R., Jr. Fields White Unto Harvest: Charles F. Parham and the Missionary Origins of Pentecostalism. Fayetteville, Ark.: University of Arkansas Press, 1988.

Gardiner, Gordon P. Out of Zion and into All the World. Shippensburg, Pa.: Companion Press, 1990.

Martin, Larry E., ed. The Topeka Outpouring of 1901: Eyewitness accounts of the revival that birthed the 20th Century Pentecostal Movement. Joplin, Mo.: Christian Life Books, 1997.

W.T. Stead; "The Story of the Awakening." The Story of the Welsh Revival; pp. 59-60; Fleming H. Revell Publishers; New York, New York; Copyright © 1905.

Eifion Evan; The Welsh Revival of 1904; p. 58; Evangelical

Press of Wales; 1969.

W.T. Stead; "The Story of the Awakening;" The Story of the Welsh Revival; pp. 59 – 60; Fleming H. Revell; New York, New York; Copyright © 1905.

Mr. Evan Roberts; W.T. Stead, (ed.) The Story of the Welsh Revival (New York: Fleming H. Revell, 1905)

J. Edwin Orr; Tongues of Fire

K. Brower; The Gospel of the Kingdom

Charles Parham; Unity

About
THE AUTHOR

Tom & Susie Scarrella

Tom Scarrella is the founder/president of *Scarrella Ministries*, an international traveling ministry based out of Fort Lauderdale, Florida. Tom is also the founder and director of *Ministry Training Institute* (MTI), a correspondence based ministry training program. In addition, Tom and his wife, Susie, host their own weekly television program, *"All for the Kingdom,"* which airs in over 200 million homes around the globe.

At the HEART of *Scarrella Ministries*, revival burns. It is their passion to see the body of Jesus Christ fervently set ablaze with Grace, Truth, Miracles, and with the Power of God, reaching out to a lost world to establish the Kingdom of God among men.

Beginning in the ministry in 1986, Tom pastored until 1994 when, after transitioning their entire ministry, he founded *Scarrella Ministries* and began traveling worldwide igniting revival fires. Since their marriage in 2003, together Tom and Susie, have ministered in over twenty nations and in every one of the United States of America.

Since their ministry's inception, they have continued to minister with a strong emphasis on *Revival, Passion, and the Power of God.* As a ministry, since 2003 they have been witness to a mighty increase in miracles, signs, and wonders as unlike any other time in the history of Scarrella Ministries. As a result, thousands have been healed from blindness, deafness, lameness, and diseases. And just as with the commission of the early disciples, SIGNS and WONDERS follow their ministry.

"And my speech and my preaching was not with enticing words of man's wisdom, but in demonstration of the Spirit and of power: That your faith should not stand in the wisdom of men, but in the power of God."

I Corinthians 2:4-5

Tom Scarrella Ministries
www.SHAREtheFIRE.org
phone 954-336-5993

Made in the USA
Middletown, DE
14 January 2020